FIRST IMPRESSIONS

10/99

FIRST IMPRESSIONS

Francisco Goya

ANN WALDRON

Harry N. Abrams, Inc., Publishers, New York

SERIES EDITOR : Robert Morton

TEXT EDITOR : Ellyn Childs Allison

DESIGNER : Joan Lockhart

PHOTO RESEARCH : Neil Ryder Hoos

Library of Congress Cataloging-in-Publication Data
Waldron, Ann.
Francisco Goya / Ann Waldron.
p.   cm. — (First impressions)
Includes index.
Summary: A biography of the Spanish painter, a forerunner of the impressionist
movement, who was noted for his royal portraits, his drawings of the horrors of war, and
his politically and socially satirical etchings.
ISBN 0–8109–3368–3
1. Goya, Francisco, 1746–1828—Juvenile literature.   2. Artists—Spain—Biography—
Juvenile literature.   [1. Goya, Francisco, 1746–1828.   2. Artists.] I. Title.   II. Series:
First impressions (New York, N.Y.)
N7113.G68W35 1992
760'.092—dc20   [B]   92-7086
CIP

Published in 1992 by Harry N. Abrams, Incorporated, New York
A Times Mirror Company

Printed and bound in Hong Kong

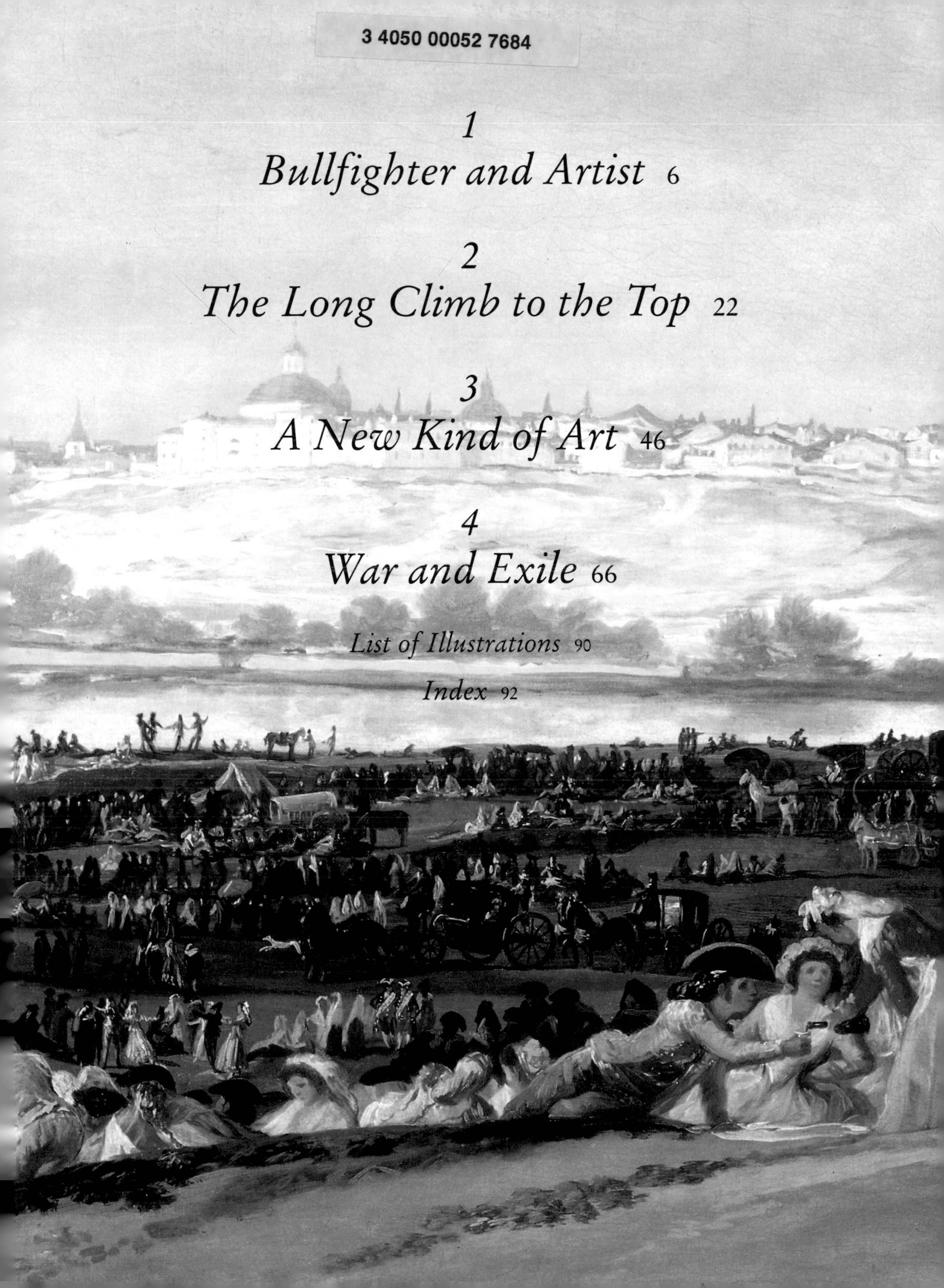

1

Bullfighter and Artist

Everything we know about Goya seems to contradict something else we know about him. He was the last of the old masters and the first modern painter. He loved to hunt and shoot birds and small animals and reveled in bullfights, but he adored dogs and children. He was a something of a social climber and longed to paint aristocrats, but he made cruel fun of the aristocracy even when he painted their official portraits. He was accused of treason during Spain's war with France, but nobody was ever a more devoted Spaniard. He attacked the Catholic church but his religious paintings have great power. He painted beautiful women, kings and queens, gypsies, children, soldiers, saints, happy people picnicking and dancing, but he also did pictures of the Roman god Saturn devouring his children, of devils, witches, and goblins, and of the unspeakable horrors of war.

SELF-PORTRAIT. About 1773
In the year before his first royal commission, and possibly
to celebrate his marriage to Josefa, Goya pictured himself as
a calm and confident young man.

But there is one fact about Goya that cannot be contradicted: He was the greatest artistic genius of his time.

He was born on March 30, 1746, in a tiny stone cottage in the village of Fuendetodos, in the province of Spain called Aragon. His parents named him Francisco de Paula José Goya y Lucientes, following the Spanish custom of joining the mother's last name (Lucientes) to the father's last name (Goya) with the word *y*, which means "and." Fuendetodos was a bleak, poor village where about a hundred people lived; it had no river, and little rain fell in that region. The dry fields around the village were bleached almost white by the sun except for a few months in the spring and early summer when the wheat crop was green.

The house where Goya was born still stands. Narrow barred windows look out over the bare countryside. The main room, a kitchen and living room combined, has a stone floor, low-beamed ceiling, and a big fireplace with a built-in stone bench on either side. The room was cool in the scorching hot summers and warm in the wintertime, even when the northeast wind, the *cierzo*, howled across the dry, rocky hills.

When Goya's mother, Gracia Lucientes, inherited the little house in Fuendetodos along with some land, Goya's father abandoned his work decorating furniture and frames with gold leaf in the town of Zaragoza, to try his hand at farming. About the time Goya was three years old, his father moved the family back to Zaragoza and returned to the work of gilding. Zaragoza, with a population of about forty-two thousand, was the capital of the province of Aragon, an important city, founded by the Romans and named for their emperor Caesar Augustus. Since the Middle Ages, artists had worked there, supported by the noble families of the region and by the Catholic church.

We don't know much about Goya's boyhood. We know he had two sisters, Rita and Jacinta, and three brothers, Tomás, Mariano, and Camillo. We know he liked to wander about the countryside and that he was a stocky, aggressive boy who got into fights and threw rocks. He liked to sing and he could dance the *jota,* the Aragonese step. There is a legend that he drew on the walls of houses and barns with pieces of charred wood, but none of those pictures remain. There are stories about how wild he was, how he liked to walk out from Zaragoza into the countryside, and how he listened to the tales of the old women about secret caves visited by the devil when the wind and moon were high. We do not know if the stories are true.

Spain was a backward country when Goya was a child. The Catholic church and the nobility owned most of the country's land and money. Spanish kings wasted all the gold that came in from the colonies in the

Goya was born in this two-story stone house at Fuendetodos, in the province of Aragon northeast of Madrid.

Americas on fruitless wars, and the rich stayed rich and the poor stayed poor. There was no middle class, just the aristocrats and the laborers, farmers, and artisans like Goya's father.

Goya went to a free primary school run by priests, and there he shared a bench with Martín Zapater, who would stay in Zaragoza but remain Goya's best friend for many, many years. Goya learned to read and write and picked up some Latin. When he was fourteen years old, a priest suggested that he study art under José Luzán y Martínez, who lived in Zaragoza. Luzán had been a painter at the royal court in Madrid, the capital of all Spain, and had studied in Naples, an important Italian city across the Mediterranean Sea. He admired the Italian painters, who set the standards for the world. In Luzán's studio, Goya mixed paints, washed brushes, and ran errands for the master. He also learned drawing, engraving, oil painting, and the tricky technique of making frescoes—paintings on wet-plaster walls. At Luzán's studio, he had a classmate, Ramón Bayeu, and got to know Ramón's older brother, Francisco, who was a full-fledged painter just back from studying art in Madrid.

The Goya family always went back to Fuendetodos for holidays, and the priest in that little village asked the teenage Goya to paint the decorations for the wooden doors of a cabinet that held the relics of a saint in a side

When he was about fourteen, Goya painted religious scenes on the doors of this wooden cabinet for the church in his hometown. On the outside (seen here) is the Virgin appearing to Saint James. The reliquary was destroyed during the Spanish Civil War in about 1936 and we know what it looked like only from a few photographs.

chapel. It was his first commission. He painted a Madonna and Children on the inside of the left door and his own patron saint, Francisco de Paula, on the right. When the doors were closed, you could see a painting of the Virgin appearing to Saint James.

Goya, at seventeen, could learn no more from Luzán, and he wanted desperately to go to Madrid and become a painter, make money, and become famous. There are legends that Goya was a member of a gang from the parish of El Pilar in Zaragoza that fought other gangs with fists, clubs, and knives. The story goes that a battle with the gang from San Luis resulted in many arrests. Goya escaped a jail term, according to

Late in his life Goya made a series of etchings to tell the history of bullfighting. But many of the prints show things that he had seen or heard of, such as Juanito Apiñani daringly vaulting over a charging bull.

this story, only by leaving Zaragoza. The truth is that it was time for Goya to leave home.

The young man from Aragon must have been dazzled by Madrid, which had three times as many people as Zaragoza. He must have been thrilled to find himself in the midst of palaces (the king's new twelve-hundred-room residence, under construction for thirty years, was almost finished) and churches, theaters and bullrings, street fairs and religious processions. The traffic alone was a sight to see—sporty two-wheeled cabriolets and big four-wheeled carriages drawn by horses or mules with bells on their harnesses. Bells in Madrid's fifty churches announced the daily services in noisy chorus. Jugglers performed in the plazas and parks among the fountains and statues, and ballad singers walked the streets. *Majos*, the young men of Madrid, dressed in black cloaks and tall hats, and *majas*, young women with black lace mantillas (shawls draped over high combs on their heads and falling down around their shoulders), strolled by, passing friars and priests, soldiers, bullfighters, and aristocrats in brocade and satin. Taverns and coffee houses buzzed with excitement, and there always seemed to be a festival underway. The most important ones were the carnival just before Lent began, when a romp called "The Burial of the Sardine" took place, and Corpus Christi week in June, when fireworks sprayed over the city.

Carlos III was king, the best king Spain was to have for years, and Madrid was prospering under his rule. He was a patient, gentle, rather sad man who hated theater and music but loved hunting. He was honest, deeply religious, and hardworking. Ready to try new ideas, he opened Spain to the Enlightenment, the new way of thinking that was exploding in France in the years before the French Revolution. Men and women of the Enlightenment questioned the absolute power of the Catholic church and believed that science could offer solutions to human problems. They thought "real" knowledge of the world was better than what they saw as the superstitions of religion. They believed in democracy and in education, rights, and liberty for all men and women. Not all the ideas of the Enlightenment took root in Spain, but there was a new atmosphere in Madrid, thanks to King Carlos III. The city for the first time had street lighting, garbage collection, good drinking water, and adequate police protection. There was talk of reforming taxes and land ownership across the whole country, and the king wanted to increase trade and industry and curb the church's power over nonreligious matters.

While there was a great deal in Madrid to amuse Goya and new ideas to stimulate him, he was ambitious to succeed as an artist. He applied for the fellowship offered every three years by Madrid's famous Real Academia de Bellas Artes de San Fernando (San Fernando Royal Academy of Fine Arts). He did not get one.

Carlos III had brought painters from other countries to Spain. Giambattista Tiepolo of Venice, the most brilliant and sought-after Italian painter of his time and a master of fresco, spent the last years of his life in Madrid. His two sons helped their aging father. The king also sent for Anton Raffael Mengs, a German-born painter who had been trained in Italy (Mengs's father is said to have locked him in the Vatican art galleries in Rome every day with a bottle of water and crust of bread and told him to "copy, copy, copy" until he learned how to paint with ease). King Carlos wanted Mengs to come to Madrid so badly that he promised him a fabulous salary, a house,

a carriage, and free passage to Spain aboard a ship of the Spanish navy, a man-of-war. When Mengs arrived in Madrid, Carlos named him as the director of the Royal Academy and placed him in charge of all art projects in the capital.

Tiepolo painted fanciful, romantic, yet naturalistic pictures in the colorful Rococo style. Mengs was a leader of the new Neoclassical school of painting, formed in reaction against the frivolity of the Rococo. The Neoclassicists painted serious pictures in grave, dark tones. Many Spaniards admired what they thought of as the "noble simplicity" of Mengs's Neoclassicism. Goya visited the studios of Mengs and the Tiepolos and saw immediately that Tiepolo was the greater painter. He realized that Tiepolo's style would be the one in which he could best express his zest for life. Goya also studied the paintings in Madrid by Diego Velázquez and

Bartolomé Esteban Murillo, great Spanish painters who had been born about a hundred and fifty years before Goya, and the work of other old masters like the Dutch Rembrandt and the Italian Titian. But his own work remained unrecognized.

In January 1766 Goya again entered the competition for a grant from the Royal Academy. Contestants had seven months, until July, to paint a picture on the subject, described in some detail as:

> Martha, empress of Constantinople presents herself to King Alfonso the Wise in Burgos, to ask him for a third of the sum with which she has agreed to ransom her husband, the emperor of Valudino, from the sultan of Egypt; and the king of Spain commands that she be given the whole sum.

The picture was to be painted in oil on a canvas six feet wide and four and a half feet high. After the contestants had submitted that picture, they had to report to the academy at eight thirty on the morning of July 22 and, in two and a half hours, paint in public an extemporaneous work on a subject that was kept a secret until they arrived. The topic this time was not quite as complicated as the one for the first picture:

> Juan de Urbino and Diego de Paredes, in Italy, upon seeing the Spanish army, discuss to which of them the arms of the Marqués of Pescara should be given.

Goya's work on the dome of Santa María del Pilar in Zaragoza has a lively reality that remains after two hundred years.

Immediately after the two and a half hours were up, the judges announced their decision. Goya's friend Ramón Bayeu won the gold medal for first prize. Francisco Bayeu, now painter to the king and a power in the Royal Academy, was one of the judges and voted for his brother Ramón. Goya did not receive a single vote. Discouraged, he settled down to study under Francisco, who took him on as an assistant.

When Goya was twenty-two or twenty-three, he decided to visit Italy. He traveled across Spain as a matador with a band of itinerant bullfighters, fighting bulls in little towns along the way, to earn money for his journey. His interest in bulls and bullfighting would stay with him all his life. He finished his trip by boat, and in Rome stayed with another artist. There are stories that Goya supported himself as a street acrobat and that he climbed the dome of St. Peter's church and carved his name at a height never before scaled by the public. We don't know whether these stories are true or not, but they give us some idea of what people thought about Goya. Another story says he got into trouble over an attempt to kidnap a nun and escaped the death penalty only after a man from Aragon interceded for him.

Goya certainly did not waste all his time on wild escapades. He studied the great paintings in the Vatican, including work by Renaissance artists like Michelangelo and Raphael, who had painted in Italy two hundred years before. Rome was a cheap place to live and Goya stayed for several years, learning from the painters around him. He painted several pictures, including a portrait in 1771 of Manuel de Vargas Machuca, who was visiting Rome, and the portrait shows that he was a conscientious craftsman. That same year he had his first real success. Identifying himself as "Bayeu's student," in April he entered a contest sponsored by the Academy of Fine Arts in Parma, a town in northern Italy. An Italian won first prize, but Goya won the equivalent of second place and high praise for his painting *Hannibal Crossing the Alps.* A French newspaper commented on "Monsieur Goya's . . . excellent handling of the brush, the warmth of expression in the eyes of Hannibal, and an air of greatness in the general's attitude." (The paper also said that Goya needed to develop "more truth" in his color.)

Bursting with pride, Goya went back to Spain. In Zaragoza, he was the local boy who had made good. That fall, the governors of the Cathedral of Our Lady of El Pilar decided to hire an artist to fresco a ceiling of the main chancel vault using the theme Adoration of the Name of God. Goya delivered a sketch for the design in three weeks and did a small fresco to show that he knew the technique. He underbid a respected painter named González Velázquez, who had tutored Bayeu. (Velázquez always resented the young upstart who got the commission.) Goya worked fast and finished the fresco in 1772. It is in the elaborate Rococo style, with choirs of angels on clouds under a golden triangle bathed in light that is inscribed with the name of God. It may be that Goya was by then in love with Josefa Bayeu, sister of Ramón and Francisco Bayeu, because some people say that his picture of the Virgin Mother was inspired by Josefa. For the fresco, the cathedral paid Goya fifteen thousand copper reales, as much money as a government official made in a year.

In 1772 he received a commission for a series of wall paintings for a chapel in the palace of the count of Sobradiel, near Zaragoza. He did two small pictures of saints—Joachim and Cayetano, for whom the count was named—

and three large scenes from the Bible.

Goya was soon Aragon's most successful painter, outstripping his former teacher Luzan. He was becoming self-confident about his work and developing an individual style, independent of Mengs's Neoclassicism and Tiepolo's Rococo. He did more work around Zaragoza, including eleven large frescoes for the church in the Carthusian monastery of Aula Dei outside the city. These illustrated Bible stories.

While he worked on the frescoes at Aula Dei, he courted Josefa Bayeu and finally persuaded her parents to let her marry him. Francisco Bayeu was enthusiastic about his sister's marriage to the rising young artist. We don't know a great deal about Josefa; she was about the same age as Goya, who was twenty-seven; she always dealt very patiently with Goya's explosive temperament; and she helped him with his career. Goya painted her portrait and shows us a pretty woman with reddish gold hair and big eyes, looking relaxed and serene. Goya always called her La Pepa, the nickname for Josefa. He must have loved her, but he also knew that marriage to Josefa would give him useful connections at court, and Goya was an ambitious artist. They were married in the parish church of Santa María in Madrid on July 25, 1773, and returned to Zaragoza while Goya finished work on the Aula Dei frescoes.

This is believed to be a portrait of Josefa Goya. But if it is, the artist has shown his wife as much younger than she would probably have looked in her late fifties since it was painted more than thirty years after their wedding.

2

The Long Climb to the Top

It may have seemed to Goya in Zaragoza that he would never become a court painter in Madrid. But in 1774, before he was thirty years old, he was on his way.

Anton Raffael Mengs was in charge of overhauling the Real Fábrica de Tapices de Santa Bárbara (Royal Tapestry Factory at Santa Barbara), which was financed with money from the national treasury and produced tapestries for the royal palaces. Fifty years before, King Philip V had started the factory in imitation of one in France. Weavers from Antwerp made the tapestries, following designs by Dutch or French painters. When Carlos III told Mengs to overhaul the factory, he also told him to use Spanish artists. Francisco Bayeu, who assisted Mengs, hired his brother Ramón and brother-in-law Goya. Their job was to create paintings, called cartoons, that the weavers could copy in silk and wool. (Nothing like the humorous sketches that we call cartoons today, these were full-size works in oil colors on canvas.)

It was one of the best artistic jobs in Spain—steady work, good pay, with a connection to the royal court in Madrid.

What more could an ambitious painter like Goya ask for? King Carlos, who was known as El Rey Cazador, the hunter-king, told Mengs he wanted no more tapestries based on mythology or the Bible, but rather on life in Spain. So the first cartoons that Goya did were hunting and fishing scenes for the palace dining room of the Escorial, where the king's oldest son, the prince of Asturias, and his wife, María Luisa, lived. The eight paintings show wild boar, quail, red owl, hunting dogs, and fishermen. The tapestries were hung in 1775.

Though these first cartoons are stiff and the people are painted somewhat awkwardly, the prince and his wife liked Goya's work and ordered more of his designs for tapestries to hang in their bedroom and in the hall at the Pardo Palace, another house they used. The royal family wanted tapestries that showed the clothes and games of their own times, and accordingly in 1776 Goya painted for the weavers pictures of picnics and of children picking fruit, flying kites, and playing with balloons. About this time he painted the large *Dance by the Manzanares River,* which shows a group of attractive young men and young women dancing on the riverbank while guitar players provide music. There is nothing stiff and self-conscious about these paintings. They are full of sunshine, bright colors, liveliness, and happiness.

Goya painted the *majos,* the tough young men from the working-class neighborhoods of Madrid who had become fashionable dandies dressed in tight knee-breeches, stockings, low-cut shoes, wide sashes, and short jackets. *Majos* and *majas,* their attractive young women companions, arrogantly strolled the streets looking handsome and beautiful, living by their wits. *Majas* danced, and *majos* played tambourines, castanets, and guitars. They were the rage of Madrid at that time and sometimes rich people, even roy-

THE PARASOL. 1777
*The bold patterns and strong colors of Goya's cartoon must have been relatively
easy for the weavers to translate into tapestry.*

alty, dressed like *majos* and *majas*. One of Goya's paintings for tapestry
designs, *The Parasol,* shows a pretty, smiling young *maja* sitting on the
ground. She wears a blue bodice and a yellow skirt. Her cloak billows
around her. She holds a fan in one hand and she has a black-and-white
puppy in her lap. A young *majo* shields her face from the bright sun with a
green parasol.

Goya also painted tavern brawlers, drunkards, gypsies, and cardsharps.
He painted pottery vendors and fruit sellers, a doctor, drinkers at a fountain,
woodcutters, and washerwomen. But the subject Goya seems to have loved

THE CROCKERY SELLER. 1778
*Goya's skill in capturing the vitality of everyday life, as in this roadside
scene of an aristocrat's coach passing a family selling painted pottery, won
him the king's praise in January 1779.*

most was children. Painting children was a new idea, and people loved it. Goya had no children then. Josefa had given birth to two boys, Eusebio and Vicente, who had died when they were babies, in 1775 and 1776, and Goya must have thought of those infants as he painted children playing soldiers, playing giants, tossing balls, gathering birds' nests, in a game of leapfrog, pushing carts, staging a mock bullfight, or wrestling.

Goya did an enormous number of cartoons for tapestries, more than sixty in sixteen years. Each one was hard work. He fastened a canvas, sometimes as big as seven feet by nine feet, tight on a stretcher and coated it with glue and then with paint to give it a smooth surface. He primed it with a pinkish neutral undercoat that had a clay base. He worked hard, struggling to paint elaborate scenes crammed with detail, hoping that this time Francisco Bayeu would smile with approval, and bring him to Mengs's attention.

Bayeu and Mengs were both conservative, and they regarded Goya as a cocky young artist whom they needed to keep in check. It took Goya a long time to rise to royal favor. For many years, he remained a hired artisan, working steadily for the tapestry factory while he dreamed of growing rich and owning land.

Still, his salary grew and he made extra money when his cartoons were approved for tapestries. *Dance by the Manzanares River* brought in as much as his year's salary. As Goya earned more money, he was generous to his relatives and his old friends. When his brother Tomás, now a gilder like their father, wanted to borrow thirty escudos, Goya gave it to Martín Zapater, to give to Tomás. He decided Tomás would pay it back more quickly if he thought it came from Zapater rather than from an indulgent brother. Zapater, who had been Goya's classmate at the parochial school,

D.BALTASAR CARLOS PRINCIPE DE ESPAÑA.HIJO DEL REY D.F.
Pintura de D.Diego Velazquez del tamaño natural, dibujada y grabada por D.Francisco G.

These two etchings show Goya's fascination with his great predecessor Velázquez. At left is his version of the seventeenth-century artist's portrait of Prince Balthazar Carlos astride an imposing, barrel-chested horse. At right Goya copies one of Velázquez's remarkable, sympathetic portraits of the dwarfs who once served as companions to youngsters in the royal family.

was now a well-to-do merchant in Zaragoza. Goya sent his family and Zapater presents all the time—clothes, sausages, and skin bags full of wine. Zapater sent him chocolate from Aragon and corn packed in glass jars.

Goya enjoyed himself in Madrid. The leaders of the Spanish Enlightenment became his friends and advisers and he shared their liberal ideas about education and reason. High-spirited and outgoing, he found special pleasure in music, playing the guitar, singing, and dancing to the folk rhythms of the *seguidilla* and *fandango.* He adored hunting and went out every chance he got to shoot every kind of game—duck, partridge, thrush, and rabbit. He loved his hunting dogs and took good care of them, tending to them personally and taking them to the veterinarian.

In addition to painting, he was busy with etching, a technique of making pictures by scratching the design with a needle on a wax-coated copper plate and then etching the lines into the plate with an acid solution; later, ink rubbed on the plate fills the etched design and is transferred to paper on a printing press. In 1778 he studied the king's art collection and copied many of the paintings by Velázquez. The great seventeenth-century Spanish painter, Goya decided, had been a close observer both of nature and of people and had been better at expressing the way people looked and felt than the artists in Goya's time. As he copied Velázquez and made etchings based on his copies, he learned some of Velázquez's techniques—his way of composing a picture, his sharp sense of the emotions of the subjects he painted, and his way of showing people very much alive. He became a

skilled draftsman and printmaker, and he found buyers for his Velázquez etchings.

PINTVRA DD. DIEGO. VELAZQVEZ.
Fue Representa a un ENANO y esta en el Palazio R.l de Ma.d grabada.
D. Fran.co Goya Pintor a 1778.

In January 1779, after the king had approved six of his cartoons, an excited Goya was taken to the palace to meet Carlos III himself. Goya showed the king, the prince, and the princess four pictures and was delighted that he got to kiss the hands of royalty. "I never had the good fortune to do that before," Goya wrote to Zapater. He was pleased with the compliments the royal family paid him on his work, and he wrote Zapater that he had never felt so fortunate. His dream of riches and land did not seem impossible.

But he had not reached his goal. When he applied for the position of Court Painter, a job that had much more prestige than painting tapestry cartoons, he was turned down. A man named Mariano Maella got the position instead. Fiercely jealous of Maella and of the other court painters, Goya referred to them as his enemies. And he was still not a member of the Royal Academy of Fine Arts. In 1779 he painted a picture that he knew would please the judges. He copied a study for a painting of the Crucifixion by Francisco Bayeu (Bayeu based his study on a painting by Mengs) and submitted a somber *Christ on the Cross* to accompany his petition for membership. The painting does not look at all like his tapestry cartoons, with their merry scenes of everyday life. But it got him into the Royal Academy without a dissenting vote. He was thirty-four years old.

By 1780, Francisco Bayeu had asked his brother Ramón and Goya to help him with some decorative paintings for the Cathedral of Our Lady of El Pilar in Zaragoza. Goya was to paint the Virgin Mary as the Queen of Martyrs on the inside of the dome. Excited, Goya wrote to Zapater and asked him to get him a "print of Our Lady of El Pilar" and some of the things he would need to set up housekeeping while he worked in Zaragoza—"a table, five chairs, a frying pan, wineskin, guitar, a roasting spit, and a lamp." "I do not need much," he said.

Bayeu did not like Goya's designs for the dome painting, and Goya was humiliated and angry with his brother-in-law. He did not want to change what he was doing and he found Bayeu's suggestions insulting. He thought his own way of painting much better than that of either Francisco or Ramón. In March 1781 the cathedral's building committee called him to a hearing to explain why he would not do what Bayeu asked. Goya said he did not want to seem arrogant but that he was no longer a menial worker. He said Bayeu had approved his designs in Madrid, and what was the fuss about? The dispute had to go to a mediator, Brother Félix Salcedo, a friar of the Aula Dei monastery. Brother Salcedo, who had known Goya when he was working on the paintings at the monastery, appreciated Goya's talents but said that Goya should humble himself and resubmit designs for Bayeu's approval, doing nothing until he had Bayeu's permission in writing. Goya was furious. He hated being criticized and he felt his *Queen of Martyrs* was magnificently painted in his own individual style. He struggled with the question: Should he keep on painting his own way or should he try to please the people in power so he could get ahead? His tension over his indecision made him seem vain and difficult. Even though he did make the changes Bayeu wanted, critics today agree that Goya's painting for the cathedral is much better than the work his brothers-in-law did there—it is painted in brilliant colors with spontaneity and freshness.

Goya demanded his pay the minute he finished the dome. The building committee paid him but said that he could not work on any of the other paintings. The committee then awarded medals to his brothers-in-law and even gave one to Josefa, but gave none to Goya. "Oh, remembering Zaragoza and painting, I burn alive," said Goya, who was angry with Francisco Bayeu for years.

But Goya's fame was spreading and as soon as he was back in Madrid he received a royal commission to paint the largest of seven altar canvases for

THE SERMON OF SAINT BERNARDINO OF SIENA. 1784 Goya shows the Italian monk preaching to Alfonso V of Aragon and a group of his courtiers.

the new Church of San Francisco el Grande (Saint Francis the Great) in Madrid. (A different artist would do each of the seven pictures.) He wrote Zapater to spread the word in Zaragoza so that all those "vile men" who had found fault with his work would know about it. It took him two years to paint *The Sermon of Saint Bernardino of Siena.* When the king at last unveiled all the paintings at the Church of San Francisco el Grande, everyone loved Goya's picture of Saint Bernardino and thought it the best of the seven. Still, Goya had a hard time getting his fee for the painting. He and two other painters received only partial payment for their work and in April 1785 they petitioned the prime minister, the count of Floridablanca, for the rest of their money. "Those three pictures weren't anything much," the prime minister said when he paid them the second installment, "but they were less bad than the others." The second installment was far less than they had expected, but it gave Goya some satisfaction that Francisco Bayeu's picture for the high altar was rejected because the prince of Asturias objected to it.

In January 1783, Goya received what he thought was the most important portrait commission of his life: to paint Prime Minister Floridablanca, the most powerful man in Spain next to the king. Goya worked hard on the portrait and was happy when he finished it, having both achieved a good likeness and pleased Floridablanca. It is a sumptuous portrait, showing the old Spanish statesman arrayed in a red satin suit with gold trimming and a silk waistcoat. Floridablanca's secretary hovers in the background and Goya himself is at the left, humbly offering his painting to the prime minister for inspection. Books, documents, and maps are on the table and the floor. One of the maps shows the imperial canal of Aragon, a project Floridablanca had sponsored. Goya wanted his portrait of Floridablanca to show off his skill as a painter and his ability to flatter a great man, but he could not keep himself from painting Floridablanca as he really was: haughty and withdrawn. The artist and Floridablanca had one pleasant chat while Goya worked on the picture, but Floridablanca never paid him. Goya was disappointed, not only about the money but also that the commission had not catapulted him overnight to fame and fortune. The disappointment was so much worse, he wrote Zapater, because he had had such great hopes.

While he was working on the Floridablanca portrait, he met the king's younger brother, the Infante Don Luis de Borbón. (Royal princes of Spain were called "Infante," and princesses "Infanta.") The Infante invited him to stay with him at his country home near Avila, northwest of Madrid, for eight weeks in August and September 1783 and again the following year. Goya went hunting one day with the Infante, who said, "This paint dauber is even more mad about hunting than I."

While at Avila, Goya painted a portrait of the Infante and his family. The Infante's wife, wearing a loose-fitting dressing gown, sits in the center of the picture while a hairdresser arranges her hair. The Infante plays solitaire and their little daughter peers at Goya, who painted himself working on the group portrait. He also painted individual portraits of the Infante; his wife; his son, Luis, aged seven; and María, aged three. Goya is said to have done each of these portraits in an hour. He was painting faster now, using shorter, quicker brushstrokes, and seldom making changes in what he painted. He did not always bother with preliminary sketches.

When Goya was leaving the Infante's estate, the family gave him money and a silver-and-gold gown for Josefa that Goya was astonished to find was worth a small fortune. Goya thought the Infante and his family were "angels" and said they let him leave only on condition that he come back once a year. Later the Infante gave a good job to Goya's brother Camillo, a priest. He made him chaplain at Chinchón, another of his estates.

THE FAMILY OF THE INFANTE DON LUIS. 1784
*Goya's painting of the king's brother and his family reveals the aristocrats in an
informal moment, though surrounded by courtiers as always. At center
is Doña Teresa de Vallabriga, the Infante's wife, having her hair done.
He sits beside her playing cards. Beside him is their eldest son and next
to him is his sister, María Teresa, staring with childish directness
at Goya himself, crouching at a canvas.*

About this time Goya met the duke and duchess of Osuna, who made their palace a meeting place for intellectuals, poets, and painters. The duchess of Osuna had a wild streak: she liked hard cross-country horseback riding, and she once dressed as a sailor to go with her husband to see some military operations on the island of Minorca. Goya painted several pictures for La Alameda, their country house outside Madrid. La Alameda had elaborate gardens with grottoes, temples, a canal with boats, and a theater where the duchess acted in plays. The duchess was beautiful, witty, and generous (she paid Goya for each preparatory sketch he did and then paid him for the finished work). Among the seven pictures we know Goya painted for the duke and duchess are scenes showing boys climbing up a greased pole to reach prizes at the top (a popular Spanish game called *la cucaña*), a woman on a makeshift swing, and a highway robbery.

These commissions helped establish Goya as the most fashionable portrait painter in Spain, and in 1784 he received one good commission after another. He did portraits, religious pictures, and allegories for all sorts of clients. In spite of this success, he wondered if he would ever get all the glory he deserved. He was pleased when he was appointed deputy director

THE DUKE AND DUCHESS OF OSUNA

AND THEIR CHILDREN. 1789

More formal than his portrait of the Infante's family is Goya's painting
of the Osunas, perhaps his most generous patrons. Along with the serious
air that such a picture required, Goya conveyed warm
family feeling—in the duke's gently bent posture and light grasp
of his daughter's hand.

of the Royal Academy's division of painting. He had to teach classes, but he knew this was a necessary step to the top of the ladder.

Although he enjoyed festivities and music, Goya had a dark side to his temperament. He might pout and sulk and rage and swear revenge when he thought his "enemies" were working against him. He complained bitterly to Josefa about the people who were keeping him from reaching the top. It was a hard time for Josefa. Her husband's ongoing quarrel with her brother Francisco was painful to her, but she was always loyal to Goya. They both grieved over Josefa's miscarriages and regretted that they had no children.

Goya could also be generous, settling an income on his widowed mother and lending his brother more money, but he was sometimes stingy. Though he knew he was a good painter, there was still a fear of failure that made him miserable and angry. Pride and his natural exuberance kept him going.

CARLOS III. 1786
Goya's informal portrait of the king in his hunting clothes shows a man with a warm and gentle nature. Only the silk sash and a medal on his chest, as well as the word rey *(king) on the dog's collar, reveals his position.*

In December 1784 one of Goya's dearest dreams was realized. Josefa bore a son, Francisco Javier, their only child who would survive. Javier became the light of Goya's eye and the center of his life.

In 1786 the king ordered Bayeu and Maella to search for the two best painters in the country to make oil paintings, frescoes, and cartoons for tapestries to decorate the royal palaces. Bayeu proposed Ramón, and Maella proposed Goya. Goya was forty years old when on June 25, 1786, he was at last named a King's Painter, at a good salary. "Finally!" he wrote to Zapater. Goya was thoroughly happy. He had what he wanted.

In 1786 he did a portrait of King Carlos in hunting clothes, showing us a small, dark-skinned, long-nosed, smiling man. As one critic has said, it is "as affectionate a portrait of royalty as the world has ever seen." But it was a very realistic portrait. Goya had begun to expose the idiosyncracies of the people he painted. Yet he prospered; there is no record of a patron rejecting a portrait because it did not flatter. He made up with Francisco Bayeu and painted his portrait also in 1786.

Goya and Josefa moved out of crowded central Madrid and bought a little house with a garden and a view of the Manzanares River. As soon as he was named King's Painter he bought a cabriolet, a light one-horse carriage that was as glamorous as a sports car would be today. There were only three like it in Madrid. Goya overturned his cabriolet the first time he took it out, hurting his right leg. He limped for months. Later he bought a more sensible and stable four-wheeled carriage drawn by two mules.

"I have arranged a very agreeable life for myself," he wrote to Zapater. "I no longer wait around in anterooms." People who wanted something from Goya came to see him now, he said. And yet, as he enjoyed his new power and fame, Goya felt the familiar doubts. "I have become old, with so many wrinkles in my face that you would no longer recognize me if it were not for my flat nose and my sunken eyes," he wrote Zapater. He was only forty-one, but he felt much older.

In spite of his awareness of advancing age, he painted two of his finest pictures in this period. *The Meadow of San Isidro* has been called Goya's first masterpiece. It is small, 17 by 37 inches. The painting shows a crowd of fashionable people gathered in the park across the Manzanares River to celebrate the feast day of San Isidro (Saint Isidore the Farmworker), patron saint of Madrid. In the background is a panorama of the city, with the royal palace on the left and the dome of San Francisco el Grande at the right. Goya painted the light and atmosphere so faithfully that it anticipates Impressionism, the style that swept Europe a hundred years later.

He also did an appealing portrait of the four-year-old Don Manuel Osorio Manrique de Zuñiga, who is dressed in a bright red suit with a wide sash. The little boy stands alone, holding a string fastened to the claw of a magpie. (In its beak the bird holds Goya's visiting card, decorated with palette and brushes.) Two beady-eyed cats stare—as wild beasts do in the terrifying dreams of childhood—at the bird. Every viewer wonders: What awful thing will happen next?

Goya, who sometimes worked for ten hours at a time, was so busy that the king provided him with a secretary to handle his letters and an assistant to grind his paints. The king and the royal family kept him busy, but he worked for other people, too. He was at the top of his profession.

The world around Goya changed in December 1788, when Carlos III died. A good king, he had made Spain stronger and richer. His son, the

prince of Asturias, became Carlos IV, and his wife, María Luisa, became queen. All the nobility kept the court painters busy painting portraits of the new monarchs. The duchess of Osuna commissioned two gigantic portraits to hang outside her palace on the night the king and queen officially entered Madrid. Other people built triumphal arches in front of their homes. The people of Madrid lit 120,000 candles, torches, and lanterns.

Carlos IV meant well, but he was rather stupid and liked gossip more than government. María Luisa was much smarter and stronger than her husband but she was cruel to him as well as unfaithful. She would promote one of her lovers, Manuel Godoy, to become prime minister, and he would be the real ruler of Spain. The new king and queen, however, were genuinely interested in art, and they liked Goya and his work. In April 1789 the king

named "Don Francisco Goya" (*Don* is a Spanish title that meant something like "Sir" in English), a Chamber Painter, a promotion from his rank of King's Painter, with a raise in pay. He painted many portraits of the royal couple. For instance, he did a picture of the king for the Academy of History, one for the University of Santiago, and one for the king's brother Ferdinand, the king of Naples. When Goya finished that one, Carlos IV put his arm around Goya's shoulder and commended him.

The year 1790 was one of the happiest in Goya's life. He was a rich man, with money invested in bank stock, and Javier was flourishing. He and Josefa enjoyed a vacation in Valencia.

The only thing that irked him was the fact that he still had to do cartoons for the tapestry factory. He was tired of tapestry cartoons. In 1791 the director of the factory complained that since Goya and Ramón Bayeu had not delivered their designs he would have to lay off tapestry workers. Goya said that none of the other painters of his rank had to supply cartoons and that he was busy with other royal paintings and was earning his salary. He managed to make everyone angry. He did not want to be arrogant, he said, and he asked for a month's leave to visit Zaragoza, promising to do better when he got back. When the king ordered a cutback in tapestry production, Goya was delighted. The last cartoons he did, in 1792, show scenes of Spanish life—women with jars on their heads, men on stilts, boys playing seesaw,

DON MANUEL OSORIO MANRIQUE DE ZUÑIGA. 1788
Goya's portrait of the young aristocrat portrays both the innocence of childhood and some of the violence and terror that lurk in imagination. Notice the cats'
malevolent focus on the pet bird.

and four young women tossing a straw dummy.

In 1792, although he was only forty-six, Goya was feeling old. His health was poor. He was having fainting spells and he complained of an old knife wound he had received years before. He was hallucinating, seeing assassins everywhere and skeletons with swords in their hands. In November he had a severe intestinal illness that made him writhe in agony. He traveled to Cádiz, where he stayed with Sebastián Martínez, a rich merchant. He managed to paint Martínez's portrait before he became even more ill, and nearly died. He lay in bed, delirious, for some time.

He recovered slowly, but in March 1793 he was ill again, this time with painful pounding noises in his head. Today doctors say he had acute inflammation of the ear with severe damage to the eustachian tube. He became deaf. As soon as he began to get better, he became paralyzed and

GOYA IN HIS STUDIO. 1790–95
As revealed in this self-portrait, Goya preferred painting in the bright light of morning. But he often added final touches to a work at night by candlelight. Here he wears a hat whose rim has metal brackets to hold candles.

THE STRAW DUMMY. 1791–92
*Tossing a person or a stuffed figure
in a blanket was a familiar pastime
at Spanish outdoor festivals. But
this scene also suggests that women
toy with men, a theme that Goya
often pictured.*

again he almost died. Doctors have hypothesized that he had Ménière's disease, polio, botulism, or hepatitis. Whatever it was, he was in black despair. Only his enormous drive and energy saved him.

Several weeks later the paralysis passed, although he was still deaf. He had no appetite and felt weak, but he could walk and climb stairs. There were awful buzzing noises in his head. He could not hear, but he soon picked up sign language.

The terrible illness, the brush with death, and the resulting deafness marked a turning point in Goya's life. Being cut off from much of everyday life because he could not hear was hard for him to bear, but his work would take on a new depth and seriousness—as well as disturbing bitterness.

3

A New Kind of Art

Goya was back in Madrid by the summer of 1793, well enough to attend a meeting of the Royal Academy of Fine Arts and to silence the rumors that his life as a painter was over. Although Goya felt isolated and lonely because he could not hear, he began to paint again. To exercise his imagination, as he put it to a friend, he did a set of paintings showing an attack on a coach by robbers, a theater fire, and a shipwreck. He also painted a madhouse. At that time it was the fashion in Spain and all over Europe to visit lunatic asylums to watch the odd behavior of patients. But during his illness, Goya had been temporarily mad himself and the painting reflects his fear and anger at his condition.

These pictures went on display at the Royal Academy and some people thought that Goya's work was not as good as it had been. They did not realize his paintings were simply different, not worse. His style was becoming

THE DUCHESS OF ALBA. 1795
Goya's friend, patron, and perhaps his lover, was one of the most beautiful and cultured women in all Spain.

even more original and more daring. He was using more contrasts of light and dark and more jagged, almost feverish, brushstrokes. His compositions were more crowded.

When Francisco Bayeu died, in 1795, the authorities asked Goya to take Bayeu's place as director of painting at the Royal Academy. He accepted the honor, but it had come too late. He was too deaf to teach. He could not even follow the business at academy meetings. Two years later he resigned and was appointed honorary director of painting.

Goya painted portraits again, including one that was his duty: Godoy, who had become prime minister, on his horse. And he painted the rich, beautiful, aristocratic duchess of Alba. With her black hair and black eyes, the duchess was so ravishing that when she walked down the street people watched from their windows and children stopped their games to stare. Her shy, serious husband was devoted to art and music, but she flirted with matadors, dressed in *maja* costume, adopted a little black girl named María de la Luz (but treated her more like a household pet than a daughter), and kept in her company, as a butt for jokes, a crippled friar, Brother Basil, who stuttered. She was a rival of the duchess of Osuna in the social world of Madrid and even competed with the queen herself for attention and lovers. She was thirty-two when she met Goya, who was almost fifty.

Goya's elegant portrait of the duchess shows her wearing an embroidered white dress with a red ribbon in her black hair, a red necklace, and a red sash. She points at the ground, where a white dog lies at her feet. He painted a picture of her music-loving husband leaning on a harpsichord, and another of the entire household—the duchess, her husband with a musical score in his hand, her mother-in-law, and a *dueña* (nurse-attendant) nicknamed La Beata. The duchess and two children tease La Beata.

Growing old, still deaf, and depressed, Goya enjoyed the beautiful duchess and her household.

Their friendship restored his self-confidence and helped him to see that he could still find pleasure in the companionship of other people. As for the duchess, she was proud to have Goya, one of the most celebrated people in Madrid, in her circle.

After the duke of Alba died, in 1796, his widow left Madrid to stay at her estate at Sanlúcar de Barrameda, at the mouth of the Guadalquivir River, facing the Atlantic. Goya went to pay his respects and stayed almost a year. During his visit he slowly came back to life. He was infatuated with the duchess and reveled in the luxurious life in the company of women. The duchess, in turn, was grateful for his friendship. The two conversed in sign language. While he was at Sanlúcar, the duchess made a new will. Instead of leaving money to rich relatives, she left it to people like her secretary and

For his great collection of etchings LOS CAPRICHOS, Goya made this self-portrait as a frontispiece. Those who knew him recognized his snub nose and deep-set eyes and described his expression as "satirical," "malign," or simply "bad-humored."

Although doctors were being trained much better during Goya's day, there were still many unqualified quacks. Goya pictures one of them as an ass, with the caption "Of What Illness Will He Die?," suggesting that the cure may be more deadly than the disease.

De que mal morira.?

her doctor. She also left Goya's son, Javier, a small sum each day for as long as he lived. Goya filled a small notebook with sketches at Sanlúcar. Only twelve pages have survived, but these tell us that Goya had a pleasant, lazy time. He drew women in different poses; the duchess was the model for three of them.

Goya also painted another full-length portrait of his companion, this time dressed in a black dress and black mantilla, and again pointing to the ground as though she expected someone to kneel before her. The duchess wears two rings. "Alba" is written on one, and "Goya" on the other. "Goya" is also written in big letters in the sand in the foreground facing the duchess. When the picture was cleaned many years later, one could see that Goya had also written the word *solo:* "Only Goya." Goya never exhibited the painting; he kept it in his home the rest of his life.

On his way back to Madrid, Goya went to Cádiz, where he painted pictures for the oratory (chapel) at Santa Cueva. When he reached Madrid, Goya began a new project, the series of a hundred drawings called *Los Caprichos*—consisting of caricatures, grotesque figures, and pure fantasy. The word *capricho* means caprice or whim, but in Goya's time it also referred to any concept that was not part of orthodox Catholicism—specifically to what Catholics thought were heresies, the principles of the Protestant reformer John Calvin. In 1796 *capricho* was beginning to take on a new meaning in reference to works of art: something creative and original rather than done strictly by the rules.

Goya worked on his *Caprichos* in pen and ink, gouache (opaque watercolor), and sanguine (red) wash. He made eighty etchings from the drawings, working on the copperplates in a newly rented studio space on San Bernardino Street.

The first drawing in the series is a self-portrait, showing Goya in a tall hat and high collar, almost winking at the world. Others are not as pleasant. They comment on politics, religion, and social life. Goya makes contemptuous fun of women. In one, a mother punishes a child while a daughter ignores a beggar woman, her own mother. Fickle women, nursemaids, prostitutes, greedy women—all come in for scathing ridicule.

All the *Caprichos* are open to interpretation. For instance, number 42 shows two men carrying asses on their backs. Some scholars say the men are peasants who must bear an asinine burden of high taxes. Other have said that the asses are the weight of animalistic stupidities that humans must carry.

Number 43, one of the most famous *Caprichos,* is *The Sleep of Reason Produces Monsters.* It is a self-portrait, showing Goya asleep at his desk, as a cat with glittering eyes crouches nearby and bats and owls swoop over him. This one etch-ing provides the theme for all the *Caprichos:* when humans allow their reason to lapse, irrationality takes over. The Enlightenment taught people to believe that reason was the only force that could rightly guide human beings, but Goya could see clearly that reason was not in command. Spanish life was corrupt, and the royal court was full of powerful but stupid leaders

Originally conceived as the title page for LOS CAPRICHOS, plate 43 was removed in favor of the self-portrait shown on page 50.

Goya's murals for the ceiling of San Antonio de la Florida show a lively group of ordinary people, with a few down-to-earth angels thrown in. At right are details of the whole scene, in which a murder trial is depicted. At left the back of the real murderer is seen, pushing his way through the crowd.

who were against all reform and feared the Enlightenment.

The *Caprichos* are far different from Goya's lighthearted and pleasant pictures of children at play; they are not designs for tapestry or pictures for churches. The artist is attacking wrongs at every level of Spanish life. His old women and prostitutes become witches and vampires. Men are shown to be asses teaching school, posing for portraits, or practicing medicine, looking like rats. Lawyers are parrots, speaking nonsense. He is particularly hard on the priests who took part in the brutal, powerful Inquisition. The

Inquisition, operating under the protection of the Spanish government, was the arm of the Catholic church that tried and punished Spaniards not only for religious heresy but for political and social crimes.

As Goya worked, his drawings grew more distorted and passionate, full of ever more fantastic creatures. Someone has said he was living out his life like a silent movie. He seems to have experienced a kaleidoscope of forms and visions that he could not put together. The court painter had become a revolutionary.

He did not abandon his more traditional work. In 1798 he finished one of his most unusual projects, frescoes for the dome in the new Church of San Antonio de la Florida, just outside Madrid's city wall, near the Manzanares River. The church, named for Saint Anthony of Padua, was built to serve poor people—customs officials, the city's gatekeepers, and washerwomen

who used the river to do laundry. The legend of Saint Anthony says that he brought back to life a murdered man so the victim could tell the truth about his murder and thus clear Saint Anthony's father, who had been unjustly accused of the crime. To paint the story in that church, Goya used an original scheme. Most painters put angels high up in the dome of a church, closest to the sky, and put the saints down below. Goya painted angels in the arches and panels of the walls below the dome and put the scene of Saint Anthony's miracle in the dome itself. Over the altar, the serious Saint Anthony brings the murder victim to life. Anthony's father, the old man standing above the corpse, looks very happy—he is about to be cleared of the murder charge. Goya demonstrates one principle of the Enlightenment—respect for the common man and woman. People watch the miracle as they lean over a railing painted around the dome. They are a mixed crowd of thieves, beggars, workers, a toothless shepherd, *majos,* and a girl in a white shawl. Dressed in the fashion of Goya's time, they seem gloriously alive. (Goya's crowds are always wonderful. Perhaps losing his hearing helped him concentrate, just as when the television sound is turned off the viewer notices more about the gestures and actions of the people on the screen.) Behind Saint Anthony, two little boys climb the railing to get a better look. The real murderer, in a black hat, tries to slip away through the crowd.

WITCHES' SABBATH. 1797–98

Goya painted six pictures for the duchess of Osuna on the theme of witches. Why the duchess, who was a great supporter of education, should have wanted these images of superstition is a mystery.

THE FAMILY OF CARLOS IV. 1800

Goya's group portrait of the royal family shows the people so honestly and makes
them look so plain that a French critic said they looked like "the corner
baker and his wife after they have won the lottery."

While he was working on the frescoes for Saint Anthony's church, Goya also painted six pictures of witches, including a *Witches' Sabbath,* for the duke and duchess of Osuna, who had a taste for the bizarre. Witchcraft was a popular subject in Spain and throughout Europe just then, and Goya painted his pictures in bright colors with a mocking tone. They were like the *Caprichos,* except they were in color.

Goya was still a painter to the king and had duties to perform. The queen wanted two portraits of herself, one in a mantilla and one on her favorite horse, Marcial. The queen was not beautiful; she was fat and had a double chin. Her face was harsh and square. Although Goya painted her just the way she looked, María Luisa did not complain about the picture, except to say she got tired posing for him. He painted the king in military uniform and in hunting clothes leaning on a gun and with a dog sitting at his feet.

In 1799 he won the most prestigious art position in Spain: Senior Chamber Painter. He began a portrait of the whole royal family, *The Family of Carlos IV,* in the spring of 1800 and finished it a year later. Painted in one of the palace picture galleries, it shows all twelve members of the royal family. Goya sketched in a thirteenth figure, the future bride of Prince Ferdinand, heir to the throne, with her head turned aside so that her features are not clear, since the match was not final. (When the prince finally married the young woman, Goya refused to paint her features into the picture because he hated retouching.) Goya is also in the picture; he painted himself on the left sketching the family. During the year he worked on the picture, he did individual sketches of the family members as well as occasional group poses. The finished painting is one of the most remarkable group portraits in the world. It shocks with its honesty. The family stands there, glittering with jewels and gold trimmings, obviously rich and powerful. Goya does not flatter them. The queen looks vicious and ugly, with her double chin, thick neck, fat arms, and square jaw. The king is fat and weak. The children fare better—they look frightened but innocent. Goya may be the only court painter brave enough to paint such a realistic portrait of a royal family. How could the family abide it? Neither the king nor the queen ever said anything about it, good or bad, but it was the last painting Goya did of them, even though he kept the title of Senior Chamber Painter. (When the painting was cleaned in 1867, a nude man appeared between two females in the frame on the wall behind the group. Goya, up to his tricks even on this occasion, had painted them out.)

From the prime minister, the brutish and widely hated Godoy, Goya also accepted commissions. He painted three medallions for the entrance of Godoy's new palace and a pair of large paintings, *Spain, Time, and History* and *The Allegory of Poetry* for the library. The subject of one of his finest portraits was the countess of Chinchón, Godoy's wife. Goya had painted her as a child, and now he showed her as an adult, and looking sad as she sat in a chair wearing a white dress and a little bonnet over her red curls. Goya also painted Godoy himself, sprawled on a sofa. He was not interested in Godoy and he did not take the trouble to do a particularly good job. Goya was getting tired. He was in his mid-fifties, he had won all the honors, earned all the money he needed, and he was in no mood to flatter a tyrant like Godoy.

Nevertheless at this time he painted two of his most famous pictures, *The Clothed Maja* and *The Naked Maja,* which were seen in Godoy's house in 1800. In these pictures, the same sultry, seductive woman lies on a sofa—in one fully dressed, in the other completely nude. Nude paintings were forbidden by the Inquisition, but Godoy hung *The Clothed Maja* so that it covered *The Naked Maja.* Legend has it that the duchess of Alba posed for both pictures, but scholars do not think she was the model. In any case, the duchess, who had lost her looks and shrunk to "skin and bones," died in 1802, when she was barely forty years old. There is some evidence that the

MARIANO GOYA. c. 1815

The grandson of the painter, born when Goya was about

sixty years old, was a joy to his eye.

model for the *Majas* was Godoy's girlfriend.

In December 1798, Goya finished *The Taking of Christ,* a full-length picture on canvas for the cathedral in Toledo. He took particular pains with it because it was to hang near *The Disrobing of Christ,* which the great Spanish artist El Greco had painted two hundred years before.

By the autumn of 1799, Goya was making plenty of money. Feeling safe and successful, he decided to publish his *Caprichos.* He printed three hundred sets and put an advertisement in the city newspaper, *Diario de Madrid,* on February 6, 1799, in which he said that painters should condemn human errors and vices in the way that poets did and that as an artist he had chosen from among the many errors and conceits approved by polite society the things that were readiest for ridicule. None of his works, he said, was aimed

Two of the most famous pictures in all Spanish art are THE CLOTHED MAJA
and THE NAKED MAJA, *believed to be modeled by a woman Manuel Godoy was
in love with but could not marry.*

at exposing the faults of any individual.

Two weeks later *Los Caprichos* went on sale in the little perfume and liquor shop below his studio. The price was one ounce of gold for each set. The duke and duchess of Osuna, who bought four sets, were among his first customers—his few customers, as things turned out. During the next four years, only twenty-seven sets were sold, in spite of the fact that Goya was Spain's leading artist. People felt the drawings were too horrible, too morbid, too fantastic, and too puzzling.

The Inquisition was at a loss as to what to do about Goya and his irreverent works. He had done beautiful religious paintings, but *Los Caprichos* looked dangerous to the church. The Inquisition decided to do nothing. In 1803, Goya sold the remaining sets to the king at a bargain price, a fraction of what they would have cost originally, and gave the money to his son Javier so he could travel abroad.

Goya and Josefa moved into a larger house. They had rich furniture—cabinets and mirrors, gilt-and-damask sofas, a library full of books,

paintings by the Italian masters Correggio and Tiepolo, and prints by Rembrandt. Goya drew his salary from the king and painted portraits of other people, fifty portraits between 1800 and 1808. In 1805 the twenty-year-old Javier married María Gumersinda, the daughter of a rich merchant. Goya's grandson, Mariano, who would become as dear to Goya as Javier, was born in 1806.

That was the year, too, when Goya painted six small panels illustrating an event that was the talk of Spain. A young Franciscan monk, Pedro de Zaldivia, captured a notorious highwayman, El Maragato, on June 10, 1806. Goya quickly dashed off the paintings that show, like a beautifully painted comic book, all the action: the attempted robbery, the friar wresting the bandit's gun away from him, throwing him to the ground, shooting at his legs when he tries to run away, then tying his hands.

Meanwhile, the world outside Madrid was falling apart. The incompetent trio that ruled Spain—Carlos IV, María Luisa, and Prime Minister Godoy—were no match for Napoleon Bonaparte, who had taken power in France. Napoleon thought Spain would be a great addition to his empire since Spain owned rich territory in America and controlled the Mediterranean. Napoleon had nothing but contempt for Spain and he persuaded Godoy to sign a treaty with France. After Great Britain defeated the combined French and Spanish naval fleets in the battle of Trafalgar in 1805, Spain tried to pull out of the alliance with France. But Napoleon persuaded Godoy to sign an agreement in 1807 that would let thirty thousand French troops march into Spain so they could attack Portugal. Then, Napoleon promised, they would divide Portugal in three parts, one for France, one for Spain, and one for Godoy personally. At the same time, Ferdinand, the oldest son of Carlos IV, was scheming to murder Godoy and his mother and get the throne away from his father. Ferdinand wrote to Napoleon asking his help and Napoleon saw his chance. Before anyone knew what was happening, he sent one hundred thousand French troops to Spain. On March 17, 1808, Carlos IV and the queen decided to escape to America, but a mob stopped them outside Madrid and they went back. The mob also found Godoy hiding in a rolled-up rug in his attic.

Ferdinand promised his father to protect him from the French if he would abdicate in his favor. Carlos IV agreed. On March 24, the prince rode in triumph to Madrid to meet Napoleon's military commander and brother-in-law, Marshal Joachim Murat, and claim the throne as King Ferdinand VII. Carlos IV was immediately sorry he had abdicated and asked Napoleon to help him get the throne back. Chaos reigned.

While Ferdinand was briefly in power, the Royal Academy asked Goya to paint a portrait of the new king on horseback to hang in the academy's meeting room. Ferdinand gave Goya only two sittings and then left for France, promising to sit again when he got back. Napoleon had summoned him to talk about the Spanish situation. He also persuaded Carlos and María Luisa, and Godoy to come. When he had them all together, they started screaming at each other. In the end, Napoleon made both Ferdinand and Carlos give up all claims to the Spanish throne and then handed it to his brother, Joseph Bonaparte, who became Joseph I. Goya, meanwhile, worked on his portrait of Ferdinand and finished it without a sitter. Ferdinand remained a prisoner in France, while Carlos, María Luisa, and Godoy were exiles in different French cities. None of them except Ferdinand would ever return to Spain.

4

War and Exile

Goya and many other Spaniards hoped that the French would bring liberal reforms to Spain. From the start, however, the French soldiers behaved with such savagery that the Spanish fiercely resisted their conquerors. Two of the Spanish royal children, the thirteen-year-old Infante, the heir to the throne, and his sister, were left behind in Spain when their parents went to France. They were living in the royal palace in Madrid when Napoleon ordered the Infante brought to France. On May 2, 1808, a crowd outside the palace saw the little prince being forced into a coach against his will. The crowd surged against the French guards. French soldiers fired at the Spaniards, enraging the crowd.

THE SECOND OF MAY, 1808. 1814

THE THIRD OF MAY, 1808. 1814

Although Goya witnessed the terrible fighting in Madrid when Spanish loyalists battled troops hired by the French (opposite) and the executions that followed (overleaf), he did not paint the scenes for another six years. When he did, they came alive as if they had been painted on the spot.

66

During Spain's war with France (1808 to 1814), Goya made many drawings of the terrible scenes he saw and heard about. He began making etchings for DISASTERS OF WAR in 1810 and completed the work in about 1823. Examples are shown below and on the following pages.

73

THE COLOSSUS. 1808–12

Behind a stormy plain, where streams
of people and animals seem to flee in terror,
a naked giant looms. The meaning of this
powerful and emotional painting has long been
debated, but it seems likely to have been
inspired by a poem published in 1808 that tells
how a guardian spirit would rise out of the
Pyrenees Mountains and save the people of Spain
from Napoleon's oppressions.

The mob was even angrier when the French brought in reinforcements that included the Mamelukes, mercenary soldiers from Egypt. The Spaniards, most of them unarmed, rushed at the Mamelukes, pulled them from their horses and attacked them with knives and bare hands. The French marshal ordered firing squads to shoot any Spaniards who had taken part in the uprising and any Spaniards found to be armed. The firing squads began their bloody work at once, without waiting for trials.

A servant said later that Goya prowled the streets of Madrid that night with a lantern, observing all that went on. Whether or not Goya witnessed the events of May 2 and May 3, six years later he painted two brilliant, historical pictures that make people who have seen them remember the dates forever. The first, *The Second of May, 1808,* shows the Spanish citizenry, on foot, struggling with the armed and mounted Mamelukes. A firing squad is at work in *The Third of May, 1808,* which some people call the greatest picture Goya painted. A victim in a white shirt holds up his hands, his face frozen in absolute terror, as the firing squad aims remorselessly at him. His comrades hide their faces, cringe in horror, or lie awkwardly on the ground, already dead. It is, as one writer said, an unforgettable confrontation between naked power and the defenseless individual. The brilliant color and the drama of the night lighting make the picture unforgettable.

The rebellion of May 2 escalated into a war for liberation that lasted six years and brought brutality, hunger, and misery to Spain. In 1809, the citizens of Zaragoza, Goya's hometown—men, women, and children, monks and priests—beat back eighteen thousand experienced French soldiers, street by street, house by house. Goya requested permission to go to Zaragoza to paint the action. He wanted, he said in his petition, to "perpetuate the most notable and heroic deeds or scenes of our glorious insurrection against the tyrant of Europe." Zaragoza's ragtag force surrendered only after two months of bitter resistance, when fifty thousand citizens had been killed in action or died of famine or epidemic disease. Goya traveled all over Spain observing and recording the brutality, the hunger, and the misery of the war. Rape, torture, mass murder, mutilation of corpses—they are all in a series of etchings, *Los Desastres de la Guerra (Disasters of War)*, that he began during the war and finished after the war was over. In one, a French soldier drags a Spanish mother away, leaving her baby crying on the ground in front of a church. There are terrifying pictures of bandits and their atrocities, burning villages, shootings, hangings, and burial pits. Goya showed French soldiers committing brutal acts, but he also showed men in Spanish uniforms doing horrible things. Goya thought it best not to publish them during his lifetime.

Toward the end of the war he painted, apparently for his own eyes, one of his most frightening and powerful pictures, *The Colossus,* which shows a huge naked man towering to the sky while behind him a crowd of tiny terrified people and horses run in all directions. Some critics believe the giant symbolizes Napoleon terrorizing the Spanish people, and others say he symbolizes war itself.

Goya's record of the war was new for him and for the world. Before Goya's time, artists had painted war as a heroic, romantic experience, but Goya painted war as the hell it is. It was quite an achievement for a sixty-two-year-old, deaf court painter, who had grown rich doing sumptuous portraits of the nobility and lively paintings of everyday life. He brought the freedom, boldness, and vitality of his earlier pictures to the terrible scenes of war. His work was as easy to understand and as stirring as poster art, and at the same time a record, like journalism, of what happened.

It is clear that Goya hated war, but his attitude toward the French is more complex. Even though his paintings of the May uprising were totally pro-Spanish, as we follow the action it is sometimes hard to see which side he was on. When Joseph Bonaparte came back to Madrid in December 1808, he forced the heads of all families to swear allegiance to him on the altars of parish churches. Thirty thousand men, including Goya, swore allegiance to the French king. Moreover, Goya continued as painter to Joseph, just as he had to Carlos IV and Ferdinand VII. He accepted a medal, the Orden Real de España (Royal Order of Spain), from Joseph and did other things that could be interpreted as pro-French, including serving on the committee to select fifty Spanish paintings for Napoleon's museums in Paris. (He and the other committee members kept putting off choosing the paintings, determined to pick the least important pictures they could find, until the tide turned in the war and the pictures could stay in Spain.) During those war years, Goya accepted every commission he got for portraits, including commissions from French officers and the Spanish who sympathized with the French, the *afrancesados,* as they were called. He made a great deal of money during the war.

One reason he was ambivalent toward the enemy was the belief he and his liberal friends held that the French would bring reforms that Spain needed desperately. Joseph Bonaparte abolished the Inquisition and shut down two-thirds of Spain's religious houses. Goya did a series of pen-and-ink drawings caricaturing the evil days of the Inquisition and another drawing that showed some of the sixty or seventy thousand monks and nuns, released from their vows, behaving like children let out of school.

Even during the war Goya continued to paint delightful, colorful pictures that furnished a kind of escape from what was happening to Spain. He did a series of gentle and sympathetic portraits of his grandson, Mariano, of Javier's father-in-law and mother-in-law, of the actress Antonia Zárate and of the beautiful Francisca Sabasa y García. He did more paintings of working people—*Water Carrier, The Knife Grinder,* and *The Forge*—as well as several versions of pretty, flirtatious girls in *Majas on a Balcony.* In 1811 there was not enough to eat in Madrid, and Goya did the only still-life pictures he ever painted—woodcock, duck, fish, and fruit—all looking as though they would make wonderful meals.

MAJAS ON A BALCONY. 1811
At times during the French occupation of Spain, life went on as usual. Goya's painting of these two flirtatious majas *and their gallant escorts echoes a happier day.*

In addition to public horror, Goya knew private grief during the war. Of the twenty thousand people who died during the winter of 1811–12 from hunger and cold, one was Josefa, Goya's wife. They had been married almost forty years and Josefa had been loyal and supportive, even when Goya quarreled with her own brother. Javier inherited the Goya home in Madrid but let his father stay on at reduced rent. From the inventory taken at that time we know that Goya was very well off. The value of his house and furniture, jewelry, silverware, paintings and prints, and cash on hand added up to a fortune. This did not include his salary from the court or the equipment in his studio. Goya, the revolutionary, was also a rich man.

As the war wore on, the Spanish army was in tatters. Great Britain had sent an army to Portugal, commanded by the duke of Wellington, to defeat Napoleon and the French. The word *guerrilla,* which literally means "little war," was used for the first time in history to describe partisan underground fighters. Spanish guerrillas cooperated with Wellington and harassed the French at every opportunity.

After the duke of Wellington defeated the French in Portugal and northern Spain he entered Madrid, on August 12, 1812. Joseph fled to Valencia, later to France. Goya, who painted whoever was in power, did three portraits of the duke. His full-length picture of Wellington makes him look cold and haughty and proud. The Iron Duke, as Wellington was nicknamed, did not like the portrait and said so. The story goes that Goya threw a plaster cast at him.

When the war was finally over, in 1814, Ferdinand VII, who had been in prison in France, where he spent his time embroidering church linens, was released. He came home to Spain in glory to take over the throne, and he passed through a triumphal arch, in which hung Goya's *The Third of May, 1808.* Very soon Ferdinand proved himself a worse king than his father—selfish, ungrateful, and dishonest. He threw out the constitution, dismissed the parliament, and restored authority to the Inquisition. Wellington's work was all for nothing. Spain had a tyrant for a king.

Goya painted four portraits of Ferdinand, all based on a single study and commissions poured in for other portraits. But trouble lay ahead.

The Inquisition found Goya's two *Maja* paintings, one of them the forbidden nude, among Godoy's belongings and charged the artist with immorality and then with collaboration with the French, the same as treason. At his "purification" trial, Goya's friends defended his patriotism and minimized his receiving the Royal Order of Spain from Joseph Bonaparte (Goya said he never wore it). Others emphasized Goya's painting the horrors of war at Zaragoza. At the trial, an Inquisition official testified that *The Naked Maja* was really an imitation of Titian, the Italian painter, and this helped Goya. Eventually, Goya was cleared by the Inquisition. He must have had friends on the panel. There were many, many "purification" trials, and thousands of other liberals were banished from Spain.

Goya occupied himself with a non-controversial subject during these troubled years, a series of forty-four etchings called *Tauromaquia (Bullfighting)*. He began the series as illustrations for a book on the history of

THE LOVE LETTER. 1811
Seen outside a city are a pretty maja *and her companion. Some historians
believe these paintings show prostitutes and their "Celestinas," the
women who made their arrangements.*

80

bullfighting in Spain. Since prehistoric times, Spaniards had fought the wild bulls that roamed the plains. Over the years, kings had from time to time outlawed bullfighting. Popes had tried to stop it and threatened to excommunicate anyone who participated. But Spaniards continued to enjoy the pageantry of the *fiesta de toros,* the celebration of the bulls. When Goya was half-finished with his illustrations of the history of bullfighting, he began to draw on his own memory of great moments in the ring. He enjoyed himself as he drew the matadors of past and present.

He drew El Cid, the legendary Spanish hero of the eleventh century, as a bullfighter. He showed the matador Juanito Apiñani leaping over a charging bull and Pedro Romero killing a bull at bay. He pictured the death in the ring of Pepe Illo, who had survived thirteen serious gorings during his thirty years of bullfighting. The audience was important in his bullfighting pictures. In Goya's day, the people were not just spectators; men and boys ran into the ring to tease the bulls and swarm around the matadors.

His drawing for the bullfighting series was superb. He had become one of the finest graphic artists the world has ever known. He could draw imaginary or realistic action with precision and with just a few strokes. He could make the etchings based on the drawings with great expertise.

Goya used some of the skills he learned in drawing to change his painting. His compositions became simpler and he showed that he could paint even a human face with fewer strokes, making his work more impressionistic and a less perfect likeness. He used a split reed as well as a brush to get different effects. He used colors sometimes for effect and not strictly in realistic ways. In 1819, when he was seventy-three, he began to learn the brand-new technique of lithography. Drawing directly on the porous stone used in the pro-

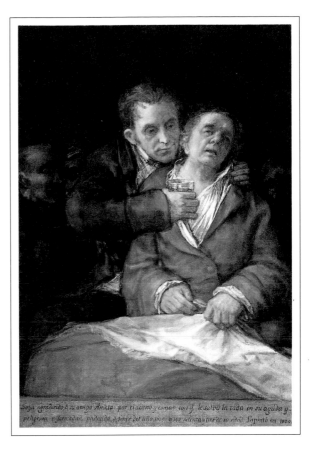

GOYA ATTENDED BY
DOCTOR ARRIETA. 1820
The artist's power of realism and
drama is nowhere so evident as in
this self-portrait recalling the way
he knew he must have looked
when he was at the edge of death.

cess, he could save the hours of scratching his picture onto a copperplate and etching the plate in acid. Lithography was not only faster than etching, it gave him great freedom of line and helped him get rich, dense blacks.

In 1819 Goya bought a country estate on twenty-two acres of land. The place was already known as Quinta del Sordo, which means "Villa of the Deaf Man," because the previous owner had also been hard of hearing. The two-story house was surrounded by a garden with a stream lined with poplar trees. Goya added wells, ponds, springs, fences, and a vineyard. Since his wife's death, he had acquired a female friend, Leocadia Weiss, who had a small daughter, María del Rosario, of whom Goya was very fond. Leocadia and Rosario lived with Goya in the country.

When Goya became ill in 1819, Leocadia nursed him, and Rosario kept him company in the sickroom. When he recovered enough in 1820 to begin painting again, he did a picture of his doctor, Eugenio García Arrieta. On the portrait, Goya wrote, "Goya thanks his friend Arrieta for the care and attention with which he saved his life in the acute and dangerous illness suffered at the end of the year 1819 at the age of seventy-three. He painted this in 1820."

When he recovered, the artist took up etching again, this time a series known as *Los Disparates,* which means "nonsense," or "blunders." The Royal Academy called the series *Los Proverbios* (*Proverbs*). Some think that

This etching from Goya's late series LOS DISPARATES shows the wild, dreamlike imagery that impelled him in old age.

Goya meant them to be called *Los Sueños (Dreams)*, because the subjects seem to be drawn from dreams and nightmares. Half-humans and other strange creatures act out scenes that floodlight the stupid and absurd aspects of marriage, poverty, war, carnival, and even bullfights.

Goya began a larger undertaking in 1820, a series of murals in oil on the white plaster walls of the dining room downstairs and in the reception room upstairs at the Quinta del Sordo. He used his brush, a palette knife, and even his fingers, to spread the black, ocher, and white paint. These paintings came to be known as his "Black Paintings" because of the despair of the subject matter. But these horrors did not frighten Goya; he may have enjoyed them, since his letters at the time are full of high spirits.

The most savage and terrifying Black Painting is *Saturn Devouring His Children.* In classical mythology, the god Saturn, alarmed by a prophecy that a son would overthrow him, swallowed each of his sons. Goya's painting shows Saturn tearing apart one of his young sons with his teeth. Another Black Painting, *The Pilgrimage of San Isidro* is in sharp contrast to Goya's earlier, bright-colored *The Meadow of San Isidro*, where joyous fashionable people enjoy the holiday with Madrid's skyline in the background. In the Black Painting, the people are close up, their faces distorted, hinting at madness. In another, the biblical heroine Judith prepares to behead the Assyrian general Holofernes. *Two Young People Laughing at a Man* make horrible faces, and *Two Old People Eating* sup on gruel. In *Witches' Sabbath,* Goya painted grotesque people crowded around a goat, who is the devil. These Black Paintings seem to indicate how Goya dealt with the emotions that tortured him: his ambivalent feelings about women, his disgust for, and perhaps also fear of, superstition and religion, his love for individual humans, and his contempt for crowds.

Late in 1823, when King Ferdinand became more despotic than ever, Goya was alarmed. He deeded his country house to his grandson, Mariano, and prepared to leave Spain. Still painter to the king, he did not want to give up his salary, so he said he was ill and asked permission to take a six months' leave of absence so he could go to a health resort at Plombières, in France.

Instead of Plombières, however, Goya went to Bordeaux, where his friends noticed that he was "deaf, old, slow, and weak," but happy and eager to see the world. He went on to Paris, where he painted portraits of Spanish exiles and did some bullfight pictures on commission. The French police kept an eye on him but found he was doing nothing subversive or wrong. He was too deaf, they said, to be a spy, and his French was so bad that he could not cause any trouble. Even though he was seventy-eight years old, he studied lithography with Carle and Horace Vernet, father and son, who taught him the latest techniques.

He did not stay long in Paris, returning in September 1824 to Bordeaux, where Leocadia and Rosario joined him. Goya adored Rosario, whom he called Mariquita, or ladybird, and taught her to draw. She played the piano and chattered to him in French. Goya took up another new skill—he began to paint miniature pictures and did forty on marble. After his leave of absence had been extended another six months, he joined other Spaniards at a café every day and, wearing a russet coat, a frilled shirt, and a top hat, talked with them of home. He may have admired the French Revolution and enjoyed French food, but he was Spanish to the bone.

When he became ill with a severe bladder infection, complicated by a tumor, he sent doctors' certificates to Madrid and was granted a full year's

SATURN DEVOURING HIS CHILDREN. 1820–23

It may be difficult to imagine living with paintings like this on the walls of your house, but Goya did.

leave of absence. When he got better, later in 1825, he did a famous series of four lithographs, *Bulls of Bordeaux.*

He went back to Madrid for two months in the summer of 1826, when he was eighty, and sat for his portrait by Vincente López, King Ferdinand's favorite court painter. He returned to Madrid again in 1827, when he formally retired and received a pension from the king. On this trip Goya also spent time with his grandson Mariano and painted his portrait again.

Although King Ferdinand seemed to have mellowed a little in the last years, Goya seemed uncomfortable in Spain and went back to Bordeaux. At eighty-one, he continued to paint and draw. Not until March 1828, did he become too ill to work. Mariano, his wife, and Javier's wife were with him, but the old man must have hoped Javier would come. On April 2, 1828, Goya woke up paralyzed completely and unable to speak. His speech

Vincente López. *Francisco Goya y Lucientes.* 1826 *This dignified late portrait of the painter was made for King Ferdinand VII. He ordered López, who replaced Goya as First Painter to the King, to pay homage to the eighty-year-old artist.*

returned, but he was unable to move again and he died on April 16, 1828. Javier was on his way, but arrived four days too late.

Goya was buried in the Grande Chartreuse cemetery in Bordeaux. Expecting Javier to look after them, he had failed to provide for Leocadia and Rosario. Nevertheless, Rosario was able to study at the Prado Museum in Madrid and became drawing teacher to Princess Isabella, who would be the next queen of Spain.

Nearly forty years after his death, in 1864, Goya's *Los Disparates (Los Proverbios)* were finally published, the same year as his *Los Desastres de la Guerra (Disasters of War)*. In 1873, Baron Frederick d'Erlanger, who had bought Goya's house, the Quinta del Sordo, had the Black Paintings taken off the walls of the villa and transferred to canvas. He later presented them to the Prado.

In November 1888, the Spanish decided that Goya's body belonged in Madrid. The Spanish consul in Bordeaux had Goya's grave opened and discovered that his skull was missing. It was like a scene from *Los Caprichos*. In 1901, the headless corpse was taken to Madrid and in 1929 his remains were transferred to the little Church of San Antonio de la Florida and buried under Goya's own frescoes of the miracle of Saint Anthony bringing a murder victim back to life. The skull was never found.

During his long, turbulent, hardworking life, Goya produced portraits that will forever mirror the people of his age, paintings that show us how sweet and beautiful life can be, and paintings and drawings that remind us of the horrors of war and human hypocrisy. Now, circling the space above his headless body is his marvelous picture of a miracle performed so that justice could be done. What more could Goya ask?

List of Illustrations

Page 51:
Of What Illness Will He Die? (*Caprichos*, plate 40). 1799.
Etching, 8½ × 5⅞".
Courtesy The Hispanic Society of America, New York

Pages 52–53:
The Sleep of Reason Produces Monsters (*Caprichos*, plate 43). 1799.
Etching and aquatint, 8½ × 5⅞".
Courtesy The Hispanic Society of America, New York

Pages 54–55:
The dome of the church San Antonio de la Florida, Madrid. 1798

Page 57:
The Witches' Sabbath. 1797–98.
Oil on canvas, 17⅜ × 12¼".
Museo Lázaro Galdiano, Madrid

Page 58:
The Family of Carlos IV. 1800.
Oil on canvas, 110¼ × 132¼".
Museo del Prado, Madrid

Page 61:
Mariano Goya. c. 1815.
Oil on panel, 23¼ × 18½".
Collection the Duke of Albuquerque, Madrid

Page 62:
The Clothed Maja. c. 1800.
Oil on canvas, 37⅜ × 74¾".
Museo del Prado, Madrid

Page 63:
The Nude Maja. c. 1800.
Oil on canvas, 37⅜ × 74¾".
Museo del Prado, Madrid

Pages 67–68:
The Second of May, 1808. 1814.
Oil on canvas, 104¾ × 135⅞".
Museo del Prado, Madrid

Page 69 (top):
Cartloads to the Cemetery (*The Disasters of War*, plate 64). 1810–1814.
Etching, 6⅛ × 8¼".
Courtesy The Hispanic Society of America, New York

Page 69 (bottom):
With Reason or Without (*The Disasters of War*, plate 2) (detail). 1810–1814.
Etching, 6⅛ × 8¼".
Courtesy The Hispanic Society of America, New York

Pages 70–71:
The Third of May, 1808. 1814.
Oil on canvas, 104¾ × 135⅞".
Museo del Prado, Madrid

Page 72 (top left):
For This You Were Born (*The Disasters of War*, plate 12). Begun 1808.
Etching, 6⅛ × 8¼".
Courtesy The Hispanic Society of America, New York

Page 72 (top right):
They Do Not Want It (*The Disasters of War*, plate 9). 1810.
Etching, 6⅛ × 8¼".
Courtesy The Hispanic Society of America, New York

Page 72:
The Colossus. 1808–12.
Oil on canvas, 45⅝ × 41⅜".
Museo del Prado, Madrid

Pages 73–74:
Barbarians! (*The Disasters of War*, plate 38).
Etching, 6⅛ × 8¼".
Courtesy The Hispanic Society of America, New York

Page 78:
Majas on a Balcony. 1811.
Oil on canvas, 76¾ × 49½".
The Metropolitan Museum of Art, New York; Bequest of Mrs. H. O. Havemeyer, 1929. The H. O. Havemeyer Collection

Page 81:
The Love Letter. 1811.
Oil on canvas, 71¼ × 48".
Palais des Beaux-Arts, Lille, France

Page 83:
Goya Attended by Dr. Arrieta. 1820.
Oil on canvas, 45½ × 31⅛".
The Minneapolis Institute of Arts; The Ethel Morrison van Derlip Fund

Page 84:
A Way to Fly (*The Proverbs*, no. 13). c. 1819.
Etching and aquatint, 9⅝ × 13¾".
Courtesy The Hispanic Society of America, New York

Page 87:
Saturn Devouring His Children. 1820–23.
Fresco transferred to canvas, 57½ × 32⅝".
Museo del Prado, Madrid

Page 88:
Vincente Lopez. *Francisco Goya y Lucientes*. 1826.
Oil on canvas, 36⅝ × 29½".
Museo del Prado, Madrid

Photograph Credits

Foto Amoretti, Parma, Italy 35; MAS, Barcelona 10, 16, 28, 32, 48; Oronoz, Madrid 1, 7, 9, 21, 25, 26, 36, 38, 41, 44, 45, 47, 55, 57, 58, 61, 62, 63, 67–68, 70–71, 72, 87, 88

Index